SELENIUM

WEBDRIVER

INTRODUCTION

BOOK 1

RAJAN

TABLE OF CONTENTS

Acknowledgement

I would like to express my gratitude to my friends and family who made their contribution to the successful publication of this book.

My special thanks to my family, friends and colleagues. I would like to thank my readers for their constant support and encouragement.

Disclaimer

This book is an independent publication and it does not affiliate or sponsored by Thought works.

Who is this Book for?

This book is intended for readers who is having keen interest to learn selenium but don't have any programming background, don't know how to start and where to start? Selenium is very vast area so I plan to explain the content in series not in single book because I don't want you to simply download some 1000 pages of selenium book and keep it in your library for few decades.

 I put all my effort to explain the contents in a most interesting way and also make the readers to understand the content by proving the screenshots and images where ever necessary.

Selenium supports several languages but in this book I'm going to demonstrate all the stuff with the help of Java language and Eclipse IDE(Because Java is the most common language and eclipse is the most popular IDE for Java language)

I assume few things from readers, you can find that below

1)You are very interested in learning selenium

2) Don't know where to start

3)Know basic core Java programming knowledge

4)You don't have any hands-on in Selenium

5)Know something about IDE(If you don't know, it's not a problem I've added images for easy understanding)

This is the first series, after reading this book you came to know how selenium works, how to work in selenium, how to automate few things in websites.

After reading this book you can't be star in Selenium but definitely it provide an insight about what are all the things you can able to automate with the help of selenium, you can easily judge whether you can able to automate your intended website or not?(In other way, checking the feasibility of your web application) and also you came to know how to automate?

Selenium tool is most commonly used by Testers and few developers for web testing. First I want to clear one thing, selenium is not a standalone software or application instead it's a kind of Java library.

1)About Selenium

Selenium is one of the renowned open source web automation tool which was initially developed by Jason Huggins in 2004 at Thoughtworks

Components of Selenium:

1)Selenium IDE

It is a complete Integrated Development environment for web testing .It is launched as an addins for the firefox .Using this IDE, tester can able to record, edit, play and debug the websites. It allow user to select the UI elements from the current page and ask to user to select the selenium commands with pre defined parameters for the UI elements.

2)Selenium client API:

It allow the user to write test script in various programming languages. These test script then communicate with selenium by calling methods in the selenium client API .Some of the supported programming languages are Java, C#, Ruby and Python.

3)Selenium Remote Control:

It is an advanced version of selenium when compared to the client API. It makes easier for the user to write test script and it currently provide client drivers for Ruby, Python, PHP, .Net, Java and Perl. It was designed by Paul Hammant. After the release of selenium webdriver, selenium RC has been officially deprecated.

4)Selenium Webdriver:

It is designed to provide a simpler and concise programming experiment by addressing some limitations in selenium Remote control. It was developed to support dynamic WebPages and advanced web application testing. The main goal of the selenium web driver is to provide a standardized API for large variety of browsers.

2)Introduction to selenium webdriver

Selenium web driver is a web automation framework. It allow the user to use a programming language to write the test script. User can use conditional operations, loop statements and much more programming techniques to design their own test script. The main aim of the selenium web driver is to automate the web applications and to make sure that the website is working as expected and it satisfies the required functionality. It contain plenty of classes and methods to meet your requirements.

Below are the list of programming languages supported by selenium webdriver

*Java

*Ruby

*Perl

*PHP

*Python

*.Net

On comparison, webdriver runs much faster than selenium RC because it directly speaks to the browser to control it.

Webdriver interact with webpage elements in more dynamic way. It allow the user to enter the text in textbox, enable the radio button, check the checkbox, select the dropdown box, click the button, submit the form programmatically and similar to what user can perform manually in the WebPages.

Below are the list of browsers supported by selenium webdriver

*Firefox driver

*Internet driver

*Html unit driver

*Andrioid driver

*Chrome driver

* Safari driver

In the above list of drivers, firefox and html unit driver is inbuilt in the selenium webdriver and for the rest of the browser a separate driver need to be downloaded from the selenium website

How webdriver works?

Humans interact with web elements like textbox, radio button, check box , button with the help of browsers but webdriver interact with web elements not only with the help of browsers but also with the help of html. Webdriver directly talks to the html of the website to do the work commanded by the programmer

When should we go for Web driver?

1)When your project contain multi browser testing

2)Working with advanced commands like Drag and drop, window pop up, alert messages etc,.

3)Facing limitations in the previous versions of selenium

3)Components Required

To automate the test script using the selenium webdriver, you need to install the below list of components

*Java

*Eclipse(*Integrated Development Environment)

*Selenium webdriver

How to install Java?

Java support all the operating Systems like windows, Linux, Mac OS etc,. Follow the below step to install Java in your machine

Step 1

Goto www.Oracle.com and choose the "Downloads" tab and select Java

Step 2

Accept the license agreement and download the Java Development Kit matches to your Operating System.

Step 3

Install the java downloaded from the Oracle websites

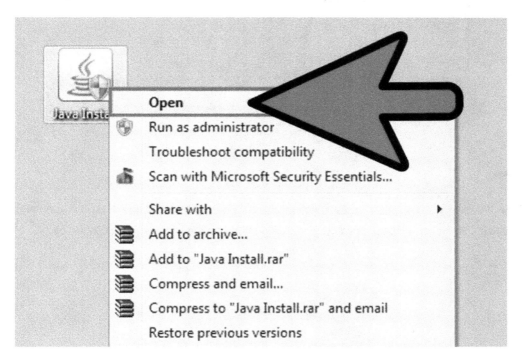

Step 4

Verify java start installing to your machine

Step 5

Goto https://www.java.com/en/download/installed.jsp and click the "Agree and continue" button, an applet will be popped out and Click on Run and know the version of your Java.

How to install Eclipse?

Step 1

Download the latest version of Eclipse IDE for java EE Developer from https://eclipse.org/downloads/ matches to your Operating system.

Step 2

Zip package will be downloaded and you need to unzip the package and install it by clicking on eclipse.exe file.

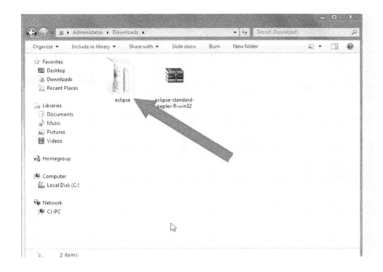

Step 3

Open the eclipse and choose the work directory(You can choose any directory)

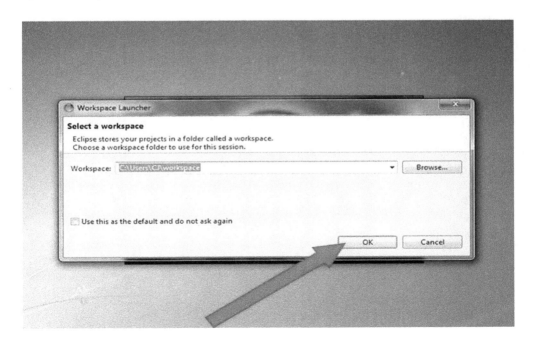

How to download selenium webdriver?

Step 1

Navigate to http://www.seleniumhq.org/download/

Step 2

Click on the Download link for Java language

While language bindings for other languages exist, these are the core ones that are supported main project hosted on google code.

Language	Client Version	Release Date			
Java	2.45.0	2015-02-26	Download	Change log	Javadoc
C#	2.45.0	2015-02-27	Download	Change log	API docs
Ruby	2.45.0	2015-02-27	Download	Change log	API docs
Python	2.45.0	2015-02-26	Download	Change log	API docs
Javascript (Node)	2.45.0	2015-02-26	Download	Change log	API docs

C# NuGet

NuGet latest release is 2.45.0, Released on 2015-02-27

4)Configuring Eclipse IDE with webdriver

You need to import the selenium webdriver to the Eclipse IDE before writing the test script

Follow the below steps to do that

Step 1

Launch the eclipse by clicking on the Eclipse.exe or from the shortcut created in the desktop

Step 2

Choose the workspace for your project by clicking the "Browse" button and click on "OK"

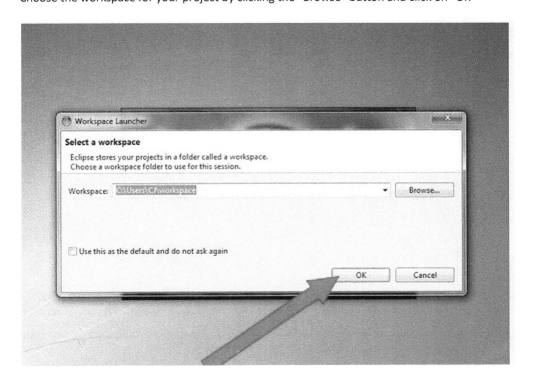

Step 3

Create New project from the File menu. File-> New->Java project

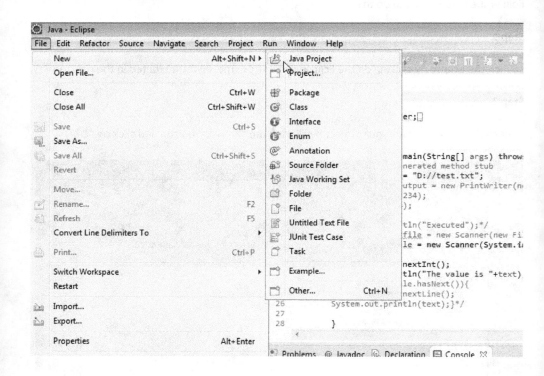

Step 4

Enter the name of your project in the project name text box. Select "Use an execution Environment" and "Create separate folders for source and class files" radio button and click Next.

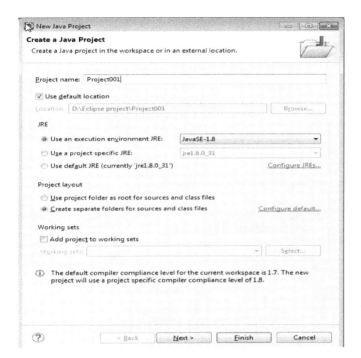

Step 5

Navigate to the Libraries tab and click "Add External Jar" button. A dialog box will appear to choose the Jar file. Choose the path where the selenium webdirver is downloaded. Include all the Jar files inside and outside the "libs" folder and finally click the "Finish" button.

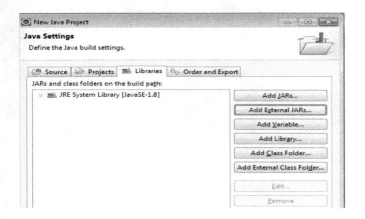

Step 6

Click on the project to create a "New" class

Step 7

Enter the class name and check the "Public static void main(String args[]") to make the class as main class.

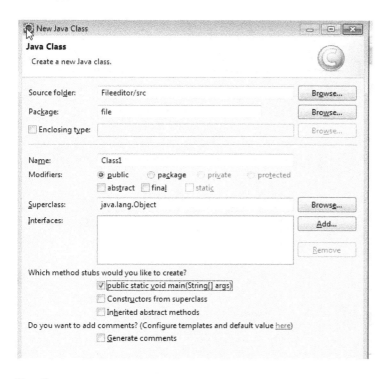

Step 8

Now the IDE is ready for programming and it will be look like image shown below

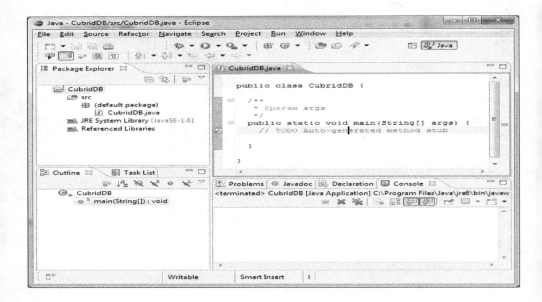

5)My First Script

Now our first task is to get the title name of the google. To do that, first we need to import the corresponding statements. In our case, we need two imports

import org.openqa.selenium.WebDriver;

import org.openqa.selenium.firefox.FirefoxDriver;

First import statement is used to refer the driver class of our selenium jar file and second import statement is used to refer the Firefox driver class.

Code:

```
try{
                    // Create a new instance of the Firefox driver

         WebDriver driver = new FirefoxDriver();
         String baseurl="https://www.google.co.in";
         String title;

// And now use this to visit Google
         driver.get(baseurl);
         title=driver.getTitle();
         System.out.println(title);

    }
        catch(Exception e){
                    e.printStackTrace();
            }


            }
```

WebDriver driver = **new** FirefoxDriver();- This statement create a new instance of Firefox driver so when this statement execute the new fire fox browser will open without any plugins.

String baseurl="https://www.google.co.in";-we assign the google url to the string variable baseurl

String title;-We declaring a variable named title to store the title of the google

driver.get(baseurl);-This statement open the url of the Google

title=driver.getTitle();-This statement get the title of the Google webpage and store the value to the variable called title

System.*out*.println(title);-This statement print the title name to the console window

We noticed that our statements are surrounded by Try and catch statements to catch the exception errors.

Our code will look like below image in the Eclipse IDE

```java
import org.openqa.selenium.WebDriver;
import org.openqa.selenium.firefox.FirefoxDriver;

public class Excercise01 {

    /**
     * @param args
     */
    public static void main(String[] args) {
        // TODO Auto-generated method stub
        try{
            // Create a new instance of the Firefox driver
            // Notice that the remainder of the code relies on the interface,
            // not the implementation.
            WebDriver driver = new FirefoxDriver();
            String baseurl="https://www.google.co.in";
            String title;

            // And now use this to visit Google
            driver.get(baseurl);
            title=driver.getTitle();
            System.out.println(title);

        }


        catch(Exception e){
            e.printStackTrace();
        }


    }

}
```

Google

6)Locating UI Elements

Web page consist of multiple web elements like radio button, check box, textbox, list box etc,. In order to control the elements we need to locate those elements first .There are several options available in the selenium to find the elements. They are

1)By ID

2)By ClassName

3)By TagName

4)By Name

5)By LinkText

6)By Partial Link Text

7)By Xpath

Now we are going to see each types in detail with case study.

1) By ID

By ID statements is used to locate the element by ID attribute and this is one of the reliable method to identify an element. But you have to make sure that our element ID is not assigned to any other elements in our webpage i.e. more than one element having same ID. If more than one element contains same ID then the selenium will target the first element identified by it.

Case Study: Now let us see how to enter the text in the google search box

To do that we need to identify the ID of the Google search text box using the inspect element technique.

Place the cursor on the Google search box in Firefox browser and right Click the mouse you will notice the inspect element field. Click on the field then the webpage source code will be displayed. The high lightened values in the below image are the source code for the Google search text box

From the above image we can able to find the ID("lst-ib") for the Google search text box. Once we identified the ID we can enter the text using the send command.

Code:

```java
import org.openqa.selenium.By;
import org.openqa.selenium.WebDriver;
import org.openqa.selenium.WebElement;
import org.openqa.selenium.firefox.FirefoxDriver;

public class Excercise01 {

    /**
     * @param args
     */
    public static void main(String[] args) {
        // TODO Auto-generated method stub
        try{

            WebDriver driver = new FirefoxDriver();
            String baseurl="https://www.google.co.in";
            WebElement text;
            driver.get(baseurl);
            text=driver.findElement(By.id("lst-ib"));
            text.sendKeys("Google");

        }

        catch(Exception e){
            e.printStackTrace();
        }

    }

}
```

We discussed most of the statements in the previous chapter. We will see the remaining statements now.

WebElement text;   This statement declare variable name text with type as webelement in order to get the control of the Google search box field text=driver.findElement(By.*id*("lst-ib"));   This statement find the element of the Google search box in the Google webpageby its ID and assign the value to the variable called text.

text.sendKeys("Google");   This statements send the text value "Google" to the text Google search text box field

2)By Class Name

Often in practical use there are many elements having same Class name so controlling the elements by class name is good practice.

Example of html class elements

```
<input id="lst-ib" class="gsfi" type="text" aria-label="Search" value=
aria-haspopup="false" role="combobox" aria-autocomplete="both" style="
auto_tion: absolute; z-index: 6; left: 0px; outline: medium none;" dir
<div id="gs_sc0" class="gsfi" style="background: none repeat scroll 0%
space: pre; visibility: hidden;"></div>
```

We will see the elements presents in one of the class name "gsfi" in the Google webpage. It doesn't have much practical use but it will show a demo for identifying elements by class name.

```
import java.util.List;

import org.openqa.selenium.By;
import org.openqa.selenium.WebDriver;
import org.openqa.selenium.WebElement;
import org.openqa.selenium.firefox.FirefoxDriver;

public class Excercise01 {

    /**
     * @param args
     */
    public static void main(String[] args) {
        // TODO Auto-generated method stub
        try{

            WebDriver driver = new FirefoxDriver();
            String baseurl="https://www.google.co.in";
            driver.get(baseurl);
            List <WebElement> getval = driver.findElements(By.className("gsfi"));

            System.out.println(getval);


        }

        catch(Exception e){
                e.printStackTrace();
            }


        }

    }
```

Problems | @ Javadoc | Declaration | Console ⊠

terminated> Excercise01 [Java Application] C:\Program Files\Java\jre7\bin\javaw.exe (Mar 27, 2015 10:54:13 PM)
[[FirefoxDriver: firefox on WINDOWS (cd3d7d9d-ac08-4b04-bab5-78a12517ba2f)] -> class name: gs

We are using the array list to get all the elements associated with class name. To use the array list we need to import java.util.List. The output is displayed in the console window below the programming window.

3)By Tag Name

Locating elements by tag name will be very helpful for tables. But as of now we will get the count of the elements having tag name as "input" in the google webpage. To get the count we need to use a method called size() i.e getval.size() which return the number of elements having the tag name "input".

Html element of tag name

```
<input id="lst-ib" class="gsfi" type="text" aria-label="Search" value=
aria-haspopup="false" role="combobox" aria-autocomplete="both" style="t
auto.tion: absolute; z-index: 6; left: 0px; outline: medium none;" dir=
<div id="gs_sc0" class="gsfi" style="background: none repeat scroll 0%
space: pre; visibility: hidden;"></div>
```

Tag name is one of the important element in the webpage and its used to define title, color and size etc. to the webpage.

Tags are used to indicate the start and end of the elements in HTML.

```java
import java.util.List;

import org.openqa.selenium.By;
import org.openqa.selenium.WebDriver;
import org.openqa.selenium.WebElement;
import org.openqa.selenium.firefox.FirefoxDriver;


public class Excercise01 {

    /**
     * @param args
     */
    public static void main(String[] args) {
        // TODO Auto-generated method stub
        try{

            WebDriver driver = new FirefoxDriver();
            String baseurl="https://www.google.co.in";
            driver.get(baseurl);
            List<WebElement> getval = driver.findElements(By.tagName("input"));
            int count=getval.size();
            System.out.println(count);
            driver.quit();


        }

        catch(Exception e){
            e.printStackTrace();
        }


        }


    }
```

Problems | @ Javadoc | Declaration | Console ⊠

<terminated> Excercise01 [Java Application] C:\Program Files\Java\jre7\bin\javaw.exe (Mar 30, 2015 8:25:12 PM)

11

4)By Name

Locating element by name attribute is one of the common methods in selenium webdriver. The name element in the html format should start with name followed by '=" sign and the name of the elements

```
rch" value="" title="Search" autocomplete="off" name="q" maxlength="2048"
th" style="border: medium none; padding: 8px; margin: 8px; height:
none;" dir="ltr" spellcheck="false"></input> ev
it scroll 0% 0% transparent; color: tra... absolute; z-index: 2; white-
```

The above Fig display the name of the google textbox as "q". Let us see how to enter the text "Got it" in the google text box field by using the name element and close the browser.

```java
import org.openqa.selenium.By;
import org.openqa.selenium.WebDriver;
import org.openqa.selenium.WebElement;
import org.openqa.selenium.firefox.FirefoxDriver;


public class Excercise01 {

    /**
     * @param args
     */
    public static void main(String[] args) {
        // TODO Auto-generated method stub
        try{

            WebDriver driver = new FirefoxDriver();
            String baseurl="https://www.google.co.in";
            driver.get(baseurl);
            WebElement getval;
            getval = driver.findElement(By.name("q"));
            getval.sendKeys("Got it");
            driver.quit();


        }

        catch(Exception e){
            e.printStackTrace();
        }


    }


}
```

5)By Link text

This method is helpful to locate an element by using the matching visible text of the link.

+You   Gmail   Images   ⠿   Sign in

In the above fig +You, Gmail and Images are the link element when user clicks on any of the link it took the user to some other URL. We can click on the link by its text name but if more than one link have same text name then the link identified first by the selenium webdriver will work.

Let us click on the link Images by using the link text method.

```java
import org.openqa.selenium.By;
import org.openqa.selenium.WebDriver;
import org.openqa.selenium.WebElement;
import org.openqa.selenium.firefox.FirefoxDriver;

public class Excercise01 {

    /**
     * @param args
     */
    public static void main(String[] args) {
        // TODO Auto-generated method stub
        try{

            WebDriver driver = new FirefoxDriver();
            String baseurl="https://www.google.co.in";
            driver.get(baseurl);
            WebElement clicklink;
            clicklink = driver.findElement(By.linkText("Images"));
            clicklink.click();
            driver.quit();


        }

        catch(Exception e){
            e.printStackTrace();
        }


    }


}
```

In the above fig we declared variable with name 'clicklink' and assign the variable to link text "Images". We used a method called click() to click the images link and it will click the link as we are doing manually.

6)By Partial Link Text

This method is helpful to locate an link element by it text but it will click any of the link if text matches partially unlike the link text method which need exact matches. Let us click on the same "Images" link by mentioning the partial text "Ima" in the partial link text method.

```java
import org.openqa.selenium.By;
import org.openqa.selenium.WebDriver;
import org.openqa.selenium.WebElement;
import org.openqa.selenium.firefox.FirefoxDriver;

public class Excercise01 {
    /**
     * @param args
     */
    public static void main(String[] args) {
        // TODO Auto-generated method stub
        try{

            WebDriver driver = new FirefoxDriver();
            String baseurl="https://www.google.co.in";
            driver.get(baseurl);
            WebElement clicklink;
            clicklink = driver.findElement(By.partialLinkText("Ima"));
            clicklink.click();
            driver.quit();


        }

        catch(Exception e){
            e.printStackTrace();
        }


    }


}
```

When we execute the above code it will click the link "Image" because its partially matches with the text mentioned in the method.

7)By Xpath

Xpath is an XML path language and it will be very helpful to identify elements in tree view structure, table format. In Xpath separate node is allocated to individual element in the tables , tree view structures etc. You can also use Xpath for other controls such as check box, links and radio button. All the browser don't have Xpath support but plugins are available for browsers to find the Xpath for elements.

For example, you can find the Xpath checker for firefox in plugins section .You can install that in your firefox by clicking on "Add to Firefox" button.

After adding the Xpath to firefox, you can identify the Xpath element by Choosing View Xpath after right clicking the mouse

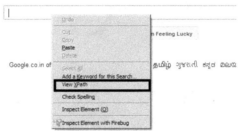

To find the Xpath of the Google text box place the cursorin the text box, right click and choose view xpath. A new window named "Xpath checker" is opened and its Xpath is displayed in the top left text box field. You can find the Xpath of the text path in the below Fig

From the Fig we can able to find the Xpath for the Google text box is "id('lst-ib')" and you can use the same to find the element.

Let us locate the text box using Xpath and send text to the text box.

```java
import org.openqa.selenium.By;
import org.openqa.selenium.WebDriver;
import org.openqa.selenium.WebElement;
import org.openqa.selenium.firefox.FirefoxDriver;

public class Excercise01 {

    /**
     * @param args
     */
    public static void main(String[] args) {
        // TODO Auto-generated method stub
        try{

            WebDriver driver = new FirefoxDriver();
            String baseurl="https://www.google.co.in";
            driver.get(baseurl);
            WebElement clicklink;
            clicklink = driver.findElement(By.xpath("id('lst-ib')"));
            clicklink.sendKeys("I find my xpath");
            driver.quit();


        }

        catch(Exception e){
                e.printStackTrace();
        }


        }


}
```

When you execute the above code it will open the new firefox browser and place text "I find by Xpath" in the google search text box and close the browser as we saw before but here we are locating the text box with the help of Xpath technique.

Conclusion

Thank you for reading this book. I hope this book definitely help the beginners to step up their knowledge in selenium and I'm sure that hereafter you are not a beginner to selenium. I feel honored to share the knowledge with my readers. I put all my effort to narrate this book in simple, easy and elusive way so that everyone can understand and grasp the content easily.

This is the first series of selenium and here I shared the info about introduction to selenium.

I have small request for you –Please leave a review for my book and feel free to tell your opinion, suggestions and corrections so that it will definitely helpful for me to improve this book and understand your need.

Regards

Rajan